The Portable Queer

OUT OF THE MOUTHS OF QUEERS

The Portable Queer series

by Erin McHugh

....

OUT OF THE MOUTHS OF QUEERS

A GAY IN THE LIFE

HOMO HISTORY

The Portable Queer

Erin McHugh

OUT OF THE MOUTHS
OF QUEERS

A Compilation of Bon Mots,
Words of Wisdom, and Sassy Sayings

alyson books
NEW YORK

MANUFACTURED IN THE UNITED STATES OF AMERICA

PUBLISHED BY

ALYSON BOOKS

245 WEST 17TH STREET

NEW YORK, NY 10011   •

DISTRIBUTION IN THE UNITED KINGDOM BY

TURNAROUND PUBLISHER SERVICES LTD.

UNIT 3, OLYMPIA TRADING ESTATE

COBURG ROAD, WOOD GREEN

LONDON N22 6TZ ENGLAND

FIRST EDITION: OCTOBER 2007

07 08 09 10 11 a 10 9 8 7 6 5 4 3 2 1

ISBN: 1-59350-032-7

ISBN-13: 978-1-59350-032-0

LIBRARY OF CONGRESS
CATALOGING-IN-PUBLICATION
DATA ARE ON FILE.

COVER DESIGN BY VICTOR MINGOVITS
INTERIOR DESIGN BY VICTOR MINGOVITS

Contents

Introduction

QUOTES ARE LIKE GOSSIP—in fact, they often are gossip. But the hard truth about what comes out of someone's mouth is this: once it's out there, it's pretty much gospel. No matter how insane, how unlikely, how ruinous it is, when it hits the ether, it becomes part of the world's anthology.

It's a shared understanding, the "that's exactly what I think, too," the "eureka" of it that appeals. A perfect quote grasps the essence of a time, a feeling, a society. So when a reader delves into one of the great volumes, like *Bartlett's Familiar Quotations*, to find the perfect thing to say—or simply to review the thoughts of The Greats who have come before him—he is bound to find a plethora of beautiful thoughts. There's not just something for everyone; there's hundreds, thousands of things for everyone.

Such is not the case in this elegant little volume. *Out of the Mouths of Queers* is by homosexuals (and their friends and nemeses), for homosexuals. So there's not something for everyone...just a lot of fabulous things

for us. Every single quote in this book was chosen because it tells a part of our history, a bit of who we are, a little of our lives. So sit back and be prepared to find out more about the queer world we live in—and probably about yourself.

The Portable Queer

LIFE

IF YOU'VE EVER

ASKED YOURSELF (AND YOU'D BE

LYING IF YOU SAID YOU HADN'T),

"WHAT'S IT ALL ABOUT?" YOU JUST MIGHT

FIND THE ANSWER RIGHT HERE IN THESE PAGES.

HISTORY'S MOST FAMOUS HOMOSEXUALS

GRIPE, PRAISE, WISH, PONDER, OPINE,

REMINISCE, REVILE, OBSESS, AND OTHERWISE

SHOUT OUT ON LIFE AND ALL ITS JOYS AND

WOES. ONE THING'S FOR SURE—THERE ARE AS

MANY DIFFERENT TAKES ON THIS THING WE

CALL LIVING AS THERE ARE PEOPLE TO LIVE IT.

"Dream as if you'll live forever.
Live as if you'll die today."

JAMES DEAN

"I shall not die of a cold.
I shall die of having lived."

WILLA CATHER

"Life was a funny thing that occurred
on the way to the grave."

QUENTIN CRISP

"You never give away your heart; you lend
it from time to time. If it were not so, how
could we take it back without asking?"

JEANETTE WINTERSON

"I love acting. It is so much
more real than life."

OSCAR WILDE

"Let life happen to you.
Believe me: life is in the right, always."

RAINER MARIA RILKE

"Live your questions now, and perhaps even
without knowing it, you will live along
some distant day into your answers."

RAINER MARIA RILKE

"The only journey is the one within."

RAINER MARIA RILKE

"The fullness of life is in the hazards of life."

EDITH HAMILTON

"Never be bullied into silence. Never allow
yourself to be made a victim. Accept no one's
definition of your life, but define yourself."

HARVEY FIERSTEIN

"I said to my dad, who's a Methodist minister,
'you know . . . one day . . . a niece or a nephew,
sooner or later we're going to get a gay or a lesbian,'
so he might as well get used to it!"

TORI AMOS

"One's real life is often the life
that one does not lead."

OSCAR WILDE

"What a wonderful life I've had! I only wish I'd realized it sooner."

COLETTE

"Is life not a hundred times too short
for us to stifle ourselves?"

FRIEDRICH NIETZSCHE

"Men for the sake of getting a living
forget to live."

MARGARET FULLER

"I have always depended on the
kindness of strangers."

TENNESSEE WILLIAMS

"Don't look forward to the day you
stop suffering, because when it comes
you'll know you're dead."

TENNESSEE WILLIAMS

"Worse than not realizing the dreams of
your youth, would be to have been young
and never dreamed at all."

JEAN GENET

"My gayness became quietly accepted and,
shock of all shocks, life went on."

LANCE LOUD

"The good we secure for ourselves is precarious
and uncertain until it is secured for all of us and
incorporated into our common life."

JANE ADDAMS

"Your joys and sorrows. You can never tell them.
You cheapen the inside of yourself
if you do tell them."

GRETA GARBO

"Without obsession, life is nothing."

JOHN WATERS

"Lesbian existence comprises both the breaking of
a taboo and the rejection of a compulsory way of life.
It is also a direct or indirect attack on the
male right of access to women."

ADRIENNE RICH

"Life
is hard.
After all,
it kills you."

KATHARINE HEPBURN

"Try and understand what part you have to play in the world in which you live. There's more to life than you know and it's all happening out there. Discover what part you can play and then go for it."

IAN MCKELLEN

"My advice to you is not to inquire why or whither, but just enjoy your ice cream while it's on your plate."

THORNTON WILDER

"There was a time when you could catch every new gay thing that came along–now we just have to pick and choose. What a wonderful luxury to have."

ARMISTEAD MAUPIN

"Your position never gives you the right to command. It only imposes on you the duty of so living your life that others can receive your orders without being humiliated."

DAG HAMMARSKJÖLD

"Morbid? You make me laugh.
This life I write and draw and portray is life as it is,
and therefore you call it morbid. Look at my life.
Look at the life around me. Where is this beauty
that I am supposed to miss? The nice episodes
that others depict? Is not everything morbid?
I mean the life of people stripped of their masks.
Where are the relieving features? Often I sit down
to work at my drawing board, at my typewriter.
All of a sudden my joy is gone. I feel tired of it
all because, I think, 'What's the use?' Today we
are, tomorrow dead. We are born and don't know
why. We live and suffer and strive, envious or
envied. We love, we hate, we work, we admire,
we despise. . . .Why? And we die, and no one
will ever know that we have been born."

DJUNA BARNES

"The longest journey of any person
is the journey inward."

DAG HAMMARSKJÖLD

"Do not seek death. Death will find you. But seek the
road which makes death a fulfillment."

DAG HAMMARSKJÖLD

"I don't know why we are here, but I'm pretty sure
that it is not in order to enjoy ourselves."

LUDWIG WITTGENSTEIN

"You've never seen death?
Look in the mirror every day and you will see it
like bees working in a glass hive."

JEAN COCTEAU

"To achieve great things, two things are needed:
a plan, and not quite enough time."

LEONARD BERNSTEIN

"Each has his past shut in him like the
leaves of a book known to him by his heart,
and his friends can only read the title."

VIRGINIA WOOLF

"Life is easy to chronicle,
but bewildering to practice."

E. M. FORSTER

The Portable Queer

LOVE

"WHAT IS THIS THING CALLED LOVE?" AS THE MAN SAID. NOTHING ELSE EXISTS THAT CAN MAKE SUCH PURE HAPPINESS FEEL SO DAMN MISERABLE. HEARTS AND FLOWERS OR SIMPLY HEARTBREAK, LOVE LOST OR LOVE AT FIRST SIGHT, IT'S THAT UNIVERSAL THING THAT MAKES THE WORLD GO ROUND AND EVERY ONE OF US GO CRAZY. CAN'T LIVE WITH IT AND CAN'T LIVE WITHOUT IT, AS EVERY ONE OF THESE LOST SOULS WILL TELL YOU.

"Who, being loved, is poor?"

OSCAR WILDE

"It had to be this little incident which made me
feel again how strong my love is for you. Oh God!
How I want to see you!"

Letter from PIOTR TCHAIKOVSKY,
to Carl Davidov

"Love was always the goal,
and my point every step of the way
was that nothing is wrong with love,
no matter what flavor it comes in."

ANI DIFRANCO

"The greatest tragedy of life is not that men perish,
but that they cease to love."

W. SOMERSET MAUGHAM

"Love is a reciprocal torture."

MARCEL PROUST

"I say I'm in love with her. What does that mean?
It means I review my future and my past in the light
of this feeling. It is as though I wrote in a foreign
language that I am suddenly able to read.
Wordlessly, she explains me to myself.
Like a genius, she is ignorant of what she does."

JEANETTE WINTERSON

"Hatred paralyzes life; love releases it.
Hatred confuses life; love harmonizes it.
Hatred darkens life; love illumines it."

MARTIN LUTHER KING, JR.

"Love is never wrong."

MELISSA ETHERIDGE

"If I was on a march at the moment I would be saying
to everyone: 'Be honest with each other. Admit there
are limitless possibilities in relationships, and love as
many people as you can in whatever way you want,
and get rid of your inhibitions, and we'll all be happy."

IAN MCKELLEN

"A man can be happy with any woman
as long as he does not love her."

OSCAR WILDE

"The important thing is not the object of love,
but the emotion itself."

GORE VIDAL

"I am tired, beloved, of chafing my heart against
the want of you; of squeezing it into little ink drops,
and posting it. And I scald alone, here,
under the fire of the great moon."

AMY LOWELL

"You are ice and fire the touch of you
burns my hands like snow."

AMY LOWELL

"He was my North, my South, my East and West,
My working week and Sunday rest,
My noon, my midnight, my talk, my song;
I thought that love would last forever:
I was wrong."

W.H. AUDEN

"I am the love that dare not speak its name."

LORD ALFRED DOUGLAS

"The love that previously dared not
speak its name has now grown
hoarse from screaming it."

ROBERT BRUSTEIN

"There is only one real deprivation. . .
and that is not to be able to give
one's gifts to those one loves most."

MAY SARTON

"Only as I am can I love you as you are."

W.H. AUDEN

"Thousands have lived without love,
not one without water."

W.H. AUDEN

"The most exciting thing is not doing it.
If you fall in love with someone and never
do it, it's much more exciting."

ANDY WARHOL

"There's this illusion that homosexuals
have sex and heterosexuals fall in love.
That's completely untrue.
Everybody wants to be loved."

BOY GEORGE

"There is a land of the living and
a land of the dead and the bridge is love,
the only survival, the only meaning."

THORNTON WILDER

"I know exactly how that is.
To love somebody who doesn't deserve it.
Because they are all you have. Because
any attention is better than no attention."

AUGUSTEN BURROUGHS

"Everybody's journey is individual. If you fall in love
with a boy, you fall in love with a boy. The fact that
many Americans consider it a disease says more
about them than it does about homosexuality."

JAMES BALDWIN

"The most important things to do in the world
are to get something to eat, something to drink,
and somebody to love you."

BRENDAN BEHAN

"It seems to me that the real clue to your
sex-orientation lies in your romantic feelings rather
than in your sexual feelings. If you are really gay,
you are able to fall in love with a man,
not just enjoy having sex with him."

CHRISTOPHER ISHERWOOD

"To be sensual, I think, is to respect and rejoice
in the force of life, of life itself, and to be
present in all that one does, from the
effort of loving to the making of bread."

JAMES BALDWIN

"Anyone who thinks that love needs
to be cured has not experienced enough
of it in their own lives."

JOAN GARRY

"Lovers may be—and indeed generally are—
enemies, but they never can be friends,
because there must always be a spice of jealousy
and a something of Self in all their speculations."

LORD BYRON

"Man's love is of man's life a part;
it is a woman's whole existence.
In her first passion, a woman loves her lover,
in all the others all she loves is love."

LORD BYRON

"Men love in haste, but they detest at leisure."

LORD BYRON

"People who are having a love-sex relationship are
continuously lying to each other because the very
nature of the relationship demands that they do,
because you have to make a love object of this person,
which means that you editorialize about them. You
cut out what you don't want to see, you add this if it
isn't there. And so therefore you're building a lie."

TRUMAN CAPOTE

"The giving of love is an education in itself."

ELEANOR ROOSEVELT

"I am not a lesbian, I just loved Thelma."

DJUNA BARNES

"All love is original, no matter how many other
people have loved before."

GEORGE WEINBERG

"Love is the big booming beat which
covers up the noise of hate."

MARGARET CHO

"It is explained that all relationships
require a little give and take. This is untrue.
Any partnership demands that we give
and give and give and at the last,
as we flop into our graves exhausted,
we are told that we didn't give enough."

QUENTIN CRISP

"Where there is great love there are
always miracles."

WILLA CATHER

"I like dogs better [than people]. They give you unconditional love. They either lick your face or bite you, but you always know where they're coming from. With people, you never know which ones will bite. The difference between dogs and men is that you know where dogs sleep at night."

GREG LOUGANIS

"No government has the right to tell its citizens when or whom to love. The only queer people are those who don't love anybody."

RITA MAE BROWN

"For one human being to love another; that is perhaps the most difficult of all our tasks, the ultimate, the last test and proof, the work for which all other work is but preparation."

RAINER MARIA RILKE

"The only queer people are those who don't love anybody."

RITA MAE BROWN

"This is the miracle that happens every time
to those who really love: the more they give,
the more they possess."

RAINER MARIA RILKE

"Who has not sat before his own
heart's curtain? It lifts: and the scenery
is falling apart."

RAINER MARIA RILKE

"[The lover says:] How beautiful you are,
now that you love me."

MARLENE DIETRICH

"How do you know love is gone? If you said that you
would be there at seven and you get there by nine,
and he or she has not called the police yet—it's gone."

MARLENE DIETRICH

"Grumbling is the death of love."

MARLENE DIETRICH

The Portable Queer

SEX

IT'S THE LUSTY

SIDE OF LOVE, THE ONE THAT KEEPS ZIPPERS DOWN AND JAILHOUSES OPEN. MAYBE IT'S JUST THAT THOSE OF US WHO ARE OUT ARE ALSO MORE OUT THERE, BUT YOU'D HAVE TO GO A FAR PIECE TO FIND A SELECTION OF FUNNIER TAKES ON "DOING THE DO" THAN YOU'LL FIND IN THESE PAGES. IT SEEMS THAT BEING ON THE WRONG SIDE OF THE SEXUAL TRACKS FOR SO LONG HAS MADE US MORE IRREVERENT THAN THE REST OF THE WORLD. BUT THE TRUTH IS THAT SEX, LIKE LOVE, IS ABSOLUTELY UNIVERSAL. MAYBE WE JUST MAKE IT FUNNIER.

"Some women can't say the word
lesbian. . . even when their mouth
is full of one."

KATE CLINTON

"I am for those who believe in loose
delights, I share the midnight orgies of
young men, I dance with the dancers
and drink with the drinkers."

WALT WHITMAN

"The dirtiest book of all is the expurgated book."

WALT WHITMAN

"When authorities warn you of the sinfulness of sex,
there is an important lesson to be learned.
Do not have sex with the authorities."

MATT GROENING

"Pleasure's a sin, and sometimes
Sin's a pleasure."

LORD BYRON

"Sometimes I wonder if men and women really suit each other. Perhaps they should live next door and just visit now and then."

KATHARINE HEPBURN

"If you're given a choice between money and sex appeal, take the money. As you get older, the money will become your sex appeal."

KATHARINE HEPBURN

"Sex is the only thing worth living for."

ROBERT MAPPLETHORPE

"Whenever you make love to someone, there should be three people involved–you, the other person, and the devil."

ROBERT MAPPLETHORPE

"I thank God I was raised Catholic, so sex will always be dirty."

JOHN WATERS

"Let my lusts be my ruin, then, since all else is a fake and a mockery."

HART CRANE

"Sexual love is the most stupendous fact of the
universe, and the most magical mystery
our poor blind senses know."

AMY LOWELL

"I find it very difficult to draw a line
between what's sex and what isn't. It can be
very, very sexy to drive a car, and completely
unsexy to flirt with someone at a bar."

BJÖRK

"Remember, if you smoke after sex
you're doing it too fast."

WOODY ALLEN

"AIDS obliges people to think of sex as having,
possibly, the direst consequences: suicide.
Or murder."

SUSAN SONTAG

"I would rather have a cup of tea than sex."

BOY GEORGE

"I never miss a chance to have sex or appear on television."

GORE VIDAL

"In homosexual sex you know exactly
what the other person is feeling, so you are
identifying with the other person completely.
In heterosexual sex you have no idea
what the other person is feeling."

WILLIAM S. BURROUGHS

"There is nothing wrong with going to bed with
someone of your own sex . . . . People should be very
free with sex, they should draw the line at goats."

ELTON JOHN

Pursuit and seduction are the essence of sexuality.
It's part of the sizzle."

CAMILLE PAGLIA

"Sex is. There is nothing more to be
done about it. Sex builds no roads,
writes no novels, and sex certainly gives no
meaning to anything in life but itself."

GORE VIDAL

"Morality is a test of our conformity
rather than our integrity."

JANE RULE

"The modern queer was invented by
Tennessee Williams. Brando in blue jeans,
sneakers, white T-shirt and leather jacket.
When you saw that, you knew they were available."

DEREK JARMAN

"I'm just having a higher level of sex [now that I'm a
celebrity]. I'm just having sex with a better grade of
person—trailer trash from only the best parks."

BRUCE VILANCH

"The big difference between sex for money and sex
for free is that sex for money usually costs a lot less."

BRENDAN BEHAN

"No matter which sex I went to bed with,
I never smoked on the street."

FLORENCE KING

"The good thing about masturbation
is that you don't have to dress up for it."

TRUMAN CAPOTE

"Erotica is simply high-class pornography;
better produced, better conceived,
better executed, better packaged,
designed for a better class of consumer."

ANDREA DWORKIN

"Concerning the Pope's claim that homosexuality
is 'unnatural.' Perhaps the Pope is suggesting that it
lies beyond the scope of 'normal' human behavior.
If so, this has uncomfortable implications for an
association of old men who wear dresses, hear
voices, and practice ritual cannibalism. Self-enforced
celibacy is all but unknown among other animal
species. If any sexual behavior is out of tune with the
natural world, it is surely that of the priesthood."

GEORGE MONBIOT

"Sex is the last refuge of the miserable."

QUENTIN CRISP

"For flavor, instant sex will never supersede the
stuff you have to peel and cook."

QUENTIN CRISP

The Portable Queer

Q

BON MOTS

WHO'S BETTER

THAN THE GAYS WITH THE SNAPPY RETORT,

THE QUICK RIPOSTE, THE BADASS VERBAL

SMACK DOWN? NO ONE, THAT'S WHO. JUST

THINK OF ALL THOSE MIKE DOUGLAS SHOWS

AND *HOLLYWOOD SQUARES*: TRUMAN CAPOTE,

BRUCE VILANCH, AND THE INIMITABLE

PAUL LYNDE. THE QUEERS HAVE IT! SO IF

YOU'RE LOOKING FOR SOME OF THE BEST

ALL-TIME ONE-LINERS, SEARCH NO FURTHER:

FROM NOEL COWARD TO FRAN LEBOWITZ TO

DAVID SEDARIS AND MORE, HERE ARE SOME OF

THE CLEVEREST THINGS EVER SAID BY SOME OF

THE SMARTEST MOUTHS AROUND.

"If you'd been any prettier,
it would have been Florence of Arabia."

NOEL COWARD *to Peter O'Toole,
star of* Lawrence of Arabia

"It is discouraging how many people are shocked
by honesty and how few by deceit."

NOEL COWARD

"It was not Cafe Society, it was Nescafé Society."

NOEL COWARD

"I love criticism just so long as it's unqualified praise."

NOEL COWARD

Dear Miss Manners: What should I say when
I am introduced to a homosexual "couple"?
Gentle Reader: "How do you do?"
"How do you do?"

MISS MANNERS (JUDITH MARTIN)

"How can I know what I think
till I see what I say?"

E.M. FORSTER

"If you done it, it ain't bragging."

WALT WHITMAN

"I've always felt that sexuality is
a really slippery thing. In this day and age,
it tends to get categorized and labeled,
and I think labels are for food. Canned food."

MICHAEL STIPE

"I'm not homosexual, I'm not heterosexual,
I'm just sexual."

MICHAEL STIPE

"An agent is a person who is sore because an
actor gets 90% of what they make."

ELTON JOHN

"Just a pawn out-played by a dominating queen."

ELTON JOHN

"I can do anything. In *GQ*, I appeared as a man."

BOY GEORGE

"The only paradise is paradise lost."

MARCEL PROUST

"Men and women, women and men.
It will never work."

ERICA JONG

"How time flies when you's doin' all the talking."

HARVEY FIERSTEIN

"A professor is someone who talks
in someone else's sleep."

W.H. AUDEN

"A real book is not one that we read,
but one that reads us."

W.H. AUDEN

"In times of joy, all of us wished we
possessed a tail we could wag."

W.H. AUDEN

"Being a woman is of special interest to aspiring
male transsexuals. To actual women it is simply
a good excuse not to play football."

FRAN LEBOWITZ

"If you remove all the homosexuals and homosexual influences from what is generally regarded as American culture, you are pretty much left with 'Let's Make a Deal.'"

FRAN LEBOWITZ

"If your sexual fantasies were truly of interest to others, they would no longer be fantasies."

FRAN LEBOWITZ

"Success didn't spoil me;
I've always been insufferable."

FRAN LEBOWITZ

"A celebrity is one who is known to many persons he is glad he doesn't know."

LORD BYRON

"Never support two weaknesses at the same time. It's your combination sinners—your lecherous liars and your miserly drunkards—who dishonor the vices and bring them into bad repute."

THORNTON WILDER

"Ninety-nine per cent of the people
in the world are fools, and the rest of us
are in great danger of contagion."

THORNTON WILDER

"What is sauce for the goose may be sauce for the
gander but is not necessarily sauce for the chicken,
the duck, the turkey, or the guinea hen."

ALICE B. TOKLAS

"I will not take but for an answer."

LANGSTON HUGHES

"Humor is laughing at what you haven't got
when you ought to have it."

LANGSTON HUGHES

"Life is not so bad if you have plenty of luck,
a good physique, and not too much imagination."

CHRISTOPHER ISHERWOOD

"Gay marriage should be legal if just to raise
the standard of dancing at receptions."

LIZ LANGLEY

"I don't care what anybody says about me as long as it isn't true."

TRUMAN CAPOTE

"I believe in luck: how else can you explain
the success of those you dislike?"

JEAN COCTEAU

"The instinct of nearly all societies is to lock up
anybody who is truly free. First, society begins by
trying to beat you up. If this fails, they try to
poison you. If this fails too, they finish by
loading honors on your head."

JEAN COCTEAU

"When a work appears to be ahead of its time, it is
only the time that is behind the work."

JEAN COCTEAU

"If I ever completely lost my nervousness
I'd be frightened half to death."

PAUL LYNDE

"Nancy Drew was always changing her outfits. I
despised girls' clothing, I couldn't wait to get home
from school and get out of it. The last thing I wanted
to read was minute descriptions of Nancy's frocks."

ALISON BECHDEL

"I came out to my sister, and she said,
'Oh my god, you're gay! Are you
seeing a psychologist?' I answered,
'No, I'm seeing a schoolteacher.'"

BOB SMITH

"It is absurd to divide people into good and bad.
People are either charming or tedious."

OSCAR WILDE

"Scandal is gossip made tedious by morality."

OSCAR WILDE

"If homosexuality is a disease, let's all call in queer
to work. 'Hello, can't work today. Still queer.'"

ROBIN TYLER

"Give me a dozen such heartbreaks, if that
would help me lose a couple of pounds."

COLETTE

"If I can't have too many truffles,
I'll do without truffles."

COLETTE

"I only go out to get me a fresh appetite
for being alone."

LORD BYRON

"I don't care if people hate my guts; I assume
most of them do. The important question is whether
they are in a position to do anything."

WILLIAM S. BURROUGHS

"Admittedly, a homosexual can be conditioned to
react sexually to a woman, or to an old boot for
that matter. In fact, both homo- and heterosexual
experimental subjects have been conditioned to
react sexually to an old boot, and you can
save a lot of money that way."

WILLIAM S. BURROUGHS

"Walk up to the woman of your dreams.
Brush your hands lightly about your face and say,
'Let me clear a place for you to sit.'"

LEA DELARIA

"A good deed never goes unpunished."

GORE VIDAL

"A narcissist is someone better looking than you are."

GORE VIDAL

"It's not enough to succeed. Others must fail."

GORE VIDAL

"My lesbianism is an act of Christian charity.
All those women out there praying for a man,
and I'm giving them my share."

RITA MAE BROWN

"They offered me either the Queen or
the Lincoln [bedrooms]. Being from San Francisco,
the Queen intrigued me. [But] I'm doing
the Lincoln. He cut me loose."

WILLIE BROWN

"I can't help looking gay. I put on a dress and
people say, 'Who's the dyke in the dress?'"

KAREN RIPLEY

"If horse racing is the sport of kings, then drag racing
must be the sport of queens."

BERT R. SUGAR

"The more
I see of men
the more
I like dogs."

MADAME DE STAËL

"Speech happens to not be his language"
MADAME DE STAËL

"Failure is the condiment that
gives success its flavor."
TRUMAN CAPOTE

"Venice is like eating an entire box of
chocolate liqueurs in one go."
TRUMAN CAPOTE

"A conversation is a dialogue,
not a monologue. That's why there are
so few good conversations: due to scarcity,
two intelligent talkers seldom meet."
TRUMAN CAPOTE

"The quietness of his tone italicized
the malice of his reply."
TRUMAN CAPOTE

"I always hated Halloween because
it's the only day when all the normals
get to dress up like us!"

MICHAEL ALIG

"If truth is beauty, how come no one has
their hair done in the library?"

LILY TOMLIN

"The only difference between a
caprice and a life-long passion is that
caprice lasts a little longer."

OSCAR WILDE

"I like persons better than principles,
and I like persons with no principles
better than anything else in the world."

OSCAR WILDE

"The only way to get rid of a temptation
is to yield to it."

OSCAR WILDE

"Just because you are blind, and unable to see
my beauty, doesn't mean it does not exist."

MARGARET CHO

"Seven beers followed by two Scotches
and a thimble of marijuana and it's funny
how sleep comes all on its own."

DAVID SEDARIS

"My own belief is that there is hardly anyone
whose sexual life, if it were broadcast, would not
fill the world at large with surprise and horror."

W. SOMERSET MAUGHAM

"I'm not interested in being with a nobody."

ROBERT MAPPLETHORPE

"For men who want to flee Family Man America
and never come back, there is a guaranteed solution:
Homosexuality is the new French Foreign Legion."

FLORENCE KING

"Everyone is in the best seat."

JOHN CAGE

"It's amazing the clarity that comes
with psychotic jealousy."

RUPERT EVERETT

"A sobering thought: what if, at this very moment,
I am living up to my full potential?"

JANE WAGNER

"When we talk to God, we're praying.
When God talks to us, we're schizophrenic."

JANE WAGNER

"I personally think we developed language
because of our deep inner need to complain."

JANE WAGNER

"Remember we're all in this alone."

JANE WAGNER (written for Lily Tomlin)

"Reality is a crutch for people
who can't cope with drugs."

JANE WAGNER (written for Lily Tomlin)

"Delusions of grandeur make
me feel a lot better about myself."

JANE WAGNER

"Pronouns make it hard to keep our
sexual orientation a secret when our co-workers
ask us about our weekends. 'I had a great time
with . . . them.' Great! Now they don't think
you're queer—just a big slut."

JUDY CARTER

"It's better to be black than gay
because when you're black you don't
have to tell your mother."

CHARLES PIERCE

"The Lord is my Shepherd and he knows I'm gay."

TROY PERRY

"Perhaps I should have become
The Artist Formerly Known as Lesbian."

ELLEN DEGENERES

"I was raised around heterosexuals,
as all heterosexuals are. That's where us gay people
come from . . . you heterosexuals."

ELLEN DEGENERES

"I'm an openly gay trailer-trash Mexican.
How could they not love me?"

RUDY GALINDO

"There's nothing that makes you so aware
of the improvisation of human existence
as a song unfinished. Or an old address book."

CARSON MCCULLERS

"The Bible contains six admonishments
to homosexuals and 362 admonishments
to heterosexuals. That doesn't mean that
God doesn't love heterosexuals.
It's just that they need more supervision."

LYNN LAVNER

"My first words, as I was being born. . .
I looked up at my mother and said,
'That's the last time I'm going up one of those.'"

STEPHEN FRY

"I don't watch television, I think it destroys
the art of talking about oneself."

STEPHEN FRY

"An original idea. That can't be too hard.
The library must be full of them."

STEPHEN FRY

"I have never seasoned a truth with the sauce
of a lie in order to digest it more easily."

MARGUERITE YOURCENAR

"Leaving behind books is even more beautiful—
there are far too many children."

MARGUERITE YOURCENAR

"A woman can look both moral and exciting . . .
if she also looks as if it was quite a struggle."

EDNA FERBER

"He may have hair upon his chest but, sister,
so has Lassie."

COLE PORTER

"If you always do what interests you,
at least one person is pleased."

KATHARINE HEPBURN

"A woman is like a tea bag—you never know how
strong she is until she gets in hot water."

ELEANOR ROOSEVELT

"Work is a four-letter word."

MORRISSEY

"I don't like it when people say
let's leave the past and go ahead, because
a lot of the future isn't that attractive."

MORRISSEY

"I do not impersonate women. How many
women do you know who march around in
7-inch heels, 3-foot wigs, and skin-tight outfits?
Women don't wear that, drag queens wear that!
The public persona of RuPaul is just a fabulous,
eye-popping celebrity package designed
to work well in front of the camera."

RUPAUL

"Tom Cruise's attorney said that
he is going to sue anyone who claims he is gay.
In a related story, Ricky Martin's attorney
has been hospitalized for exhaustion."

CONAN O'BRIEN

"They can't censor the gleam in my eye."

CHARLES LAUGHTON

"Darling, the legs aren't so beautiful,
I just know what to do with them."

MARLENE DIETRICH

"If there is a supreme being, he's crazy."

MARLENE DIETRICH

"I've developed into quite a swan. I'm one of those
people that will probably look better and better
as I get older—until I drop dead of beauty."

RUFUS WAINWRIGHT

"I now know all the people worth knowing
in America, and I find no intellect
comparable to my own."

MARGARET FULLER

"If you want reality, take the bus."

DAVID LACHAPELLE,

"Remember, if people talk behind your back,
it only means you're two steps ahead."

FANNIE FLAGG

"Humor is the ability to see three sides to one coin."

NED ROREM

"Men are pigs, but I love pork!"

CARSON KRESSLEY

"If the world were a logical place,
men would ride side-saddle."

RITA MAE BROWN

"Lead me not into temptation;
I can find the way myself."

RITA MAE BROWN

"Euphemisms are unpleasant truths
wearing diplomatic cologne."

QUENTIN CRISP

"However low a man sinks he
never reaches the level of the police."

QUENTIN CRISP

"An autobiography is an obituary in serial form
with the last installment missing."

QUENTIN CRISP

"Judge not, lest ye be judged judgmental."

FLORENCE KING

*Movie mogul Samuel Goldwyn discussing Lillian
Hellman's* The Children's Hour
with a studio associate:

GOLDWYN: "Maybe we ought to buy it?"

ASSOCIATE: "Forget it, Mr. Goldwyn,
they're lesbians."

GOLDWYN: "That's OK, we'll make them
Americans."

The Portable Queer

WORDS OF
WISDOM

IF A WORD TO

THE WISE IS SUFFICIENT, THIS ARRAY OF

ASTUTE OBSERVATIONS SHOULD BE ENOUGH

FOR A LIFETIME. SOME OF OUR GREATEST

QUEER MINDS AND SOME OF THEIR FINEST

FRIENDS SPEAK ON TRUTH AND BEAUTY,

DREAMS AND FAILURES, REVOLUTION AND

FAITH, AND EVERYTHING ELSE THAT MAKES

LIFE THE FASCINATIN' RHYTHM THAT WE ALL

DANCE TO. NOW IF IT WERE STRAIGHT FOLKS

WHO UTTERED THESE WORDS, YOU'D BE

SEEING THEM ON COINS, STAMPS, AND

POLITICAL POSTERS. *E PLURIBUS QUEERUM.*

"A dream deferred is a dream denied."

LANGSON HUGHES

"Hatred is a coward's revenge for being intimidated."

GEORGE BERNARD SHAW

"I worshipped dead men for their strength,
forgetting I was strong."

VITA SACKVILLE-WEST

"What is beautiful is good, and who is good
will soon be beautiful."

VITA SACKVILLE-WEST

"Follow your inner moonlight;
don't hide the madness."

ALLEN GINSBERG

"I have learned more about love, selflessness,
and human understanding in this great adventure
in the world of AIDS than I ever did in the cut-throat,
competitive world in which I spent my life."

ANTHONY PERKINS

"I have learned that to be with those I like is enough."

WALT WHITMAN

"I am as bad as the worst, but, thank God,
I am as good as the best."

WALT WHITMAN

"Never apologize for showing feeling.
When you do so, you apologize for the truth."

BENJAMIN DISRAELI

"If you have knowledge, let others
light their candles in it."

MARGARET FULLER

"Male and female represent the two sides
of the great radical dualism. But in fact they are
perpetually passing into one another. Fluid hardens
to solid, solid rushes to fluid. There is no wholly
masculine man, no purely feminine woman."

MARGARET FULLER

"Beware of over-great pleasure in being popular
or even beloved."

MARGARET FULLER

"Dedicate some of your life to others.
Your dedication will not be a sacrifice. It will be
an exhilarating experience because it is an intense
effort applied toward a meaningful end."

DR. TOM DOOLEY

"The horror of class stratification, racism, and
prejudice is that some people begin to believe that
the security of their families and communities
depends on the oppression of others, that for
some to have good lives there must be others
whose lives are truncated and brutal."

DOROTHY ALLISON

"I think I would have died if there
hadn't been the women's movement."

DOROTHY ALLISON

"To measure
the man,
measure his
heart."

MALCOLM FORBES

"Those who will not reason, are bigots, those who cannot, are fools, and those who dare not, are slaves."

LORD BYRON

"Hope will never be silent."

HARVEY MILK

"Genocide begins, however improbably, in the conviction that classes of biological distinction indisputably sanction social and political discrimination."

ANDREA DWORKIN

"Diversity: the art of thinking independently together."

MALCOLM FORBES

"We are always the same age inside."

GERTRUDE STEIN

"All revolutions devour their own children."

ERNST RÖHM

"The voice of conscience is so delicate
that it is easy to stifle it; but it is also so clear
that it is impossible to mistake it."

MADAME DE STAËL

"Wit lies in recognizing the resemblance
among things which differ and the difference
between things which are alike."

MADAME DE STAËL

"Only connect."

E.M. FORSTER

"If I had to choose between betraying my country
and betraying my friend, I hope I should
have the guts to betray my country."

E.M. FORSTER

"Faith is not belief. Belief is passive. Faith is active."

EDITH HAMILTON

"Unless we remember we cannot understand."

E.M. FORSTER

"The only books that influence us are those
for which we are ready, and which have gone
a little farther down our particular path
than we have yet got ourselves."

E.M. FORSTER

"Whatever helps you sleep at night, bitch."

STEWIE GRIFFIN

"Failure is success if we learn from it."

MALCOLM FORBES

"A closed mind is a dying mind."

EDNA FERBER

"I bring out the worst in my enemies and that's how
I get them to defeat themselves."

ROY M. COHN

"The Jews have never been ashamed of being Jews,
whereas homosexuals have been stupid enough
to be ashamed of their homosexuality."

RAINER W. FASSBINDER

"Nobody will believe in you unless you
believe in yourself."

LIBERACE

"As long as men are free to ask what they must,
free to say what they think, free to think
what they will, freedom can never be lost
and science can never regress."

MARCEL PROUST

"Let us be grateful to people who
make us happy, they are the charming gardeners
who make our souls blossom."

MARCEL PROUST

"People can have many different kinds
of pleasure. The real one is that for which
they will forsake the others."

MARCEL PROUST

"A champion
is afraid
of losing.
Everyone
else is afraid
of winning."

BILLIE JEAN KING

"All our final decisions are made in a state
of mind that is not going to last."

MARCEL PROUST

"We are healed from suffering only by
experiencing it to the full."

MARCEL PROUST

"Victory is fleeting. Losing is forever."

BILLIE JEAN KING

"No one changes the world who isn't obsessed."

BILLIE JEAN KING

"A man's heterosexuality will not put up with
any homosexuality, and vice versa."

SIGMUND FREUD

"Do what you feel in your heart to be right—
for you'll be criticized anyway. You'll be damned
if you do, and damned if you don't."

ELEANOR ROOSEVELT

"Great minds discuss ideas; average minds discuss
events; small minds discuss people."

ELEANOR ROOSEVELT

"You must do the things you think you cannot do."

ELEANOR ROOSEVELT

"It is better to light a candle than curse the darkness."

ELEANOR ROOSEVELT

"It is not fair to ask of others what you are
unwilling to do yourself."

ELEANOR ROOSEVELT

"No one can make you feel inferior
without your consent."

ELEANOR ROOSEVELT

"When an individual is protesting society's refusal
to acknowledge his dignity as a human being,
his very act of protest confers dignity on him."

BAYARD RUSTIN

"When you're wrong, you're wrong.
But when you're right, you're wrong anyhow."

BAYARD RUSTIN

"What you risk reveals what you value."

JEANETTE WINTERSON

"It's true that heroes are inspiring, but mustn't they
also do some rescuing if they are to be worthy of their
name? Would Wonder Woman matter if she only
sent commiserating telegrams to the distressed?"

JEANETTE WINTERSON

"If someone says 'can't,' that shows you what to do."

JOHN CAGE

"We carry our homes within us
which enables us to fly."

JOHN CAGE

"Morals are private. Decency is public."

RITA MAE BROWN

"One of the keys to happiness is a bad memory."

RITA MAE BROWN

"What's the point of being a lesbian if a woman is
going to look and act like an imitation man?"

RITA MAE BROWN

"True realism consists in revealing the
surprising things which habit keeps covered
and prevents us from seeing."

JEAN COCTEAU

"The greatest masterpiece in literature is
only a dictionary out of order."

JEAN COCTEAU

"The extreme limit of wisdom,
that's what the public calls madness."

JEAN COCTEAU

"When peoples care for you and cry for you,
they can straighten out your soul."

LANGSTON HUGHES

"Straight Americans need. . . an education of the
heart and soul. They must understand—
to begin with—how it can feel to spend years denying
your own deepest truths, to sit silently through
classes, meals, and church services while people you
love toss off remarks that brutalize your soul."

BRUCE BAWER

"I have learned to love that which is meant
to harm me, so that I can stand in the way
of those who are less strong. I can take the bullets
for those who aren't able to."

MARGARET CHO

"Never be bullied into silence. Never allow yourself
to be made a victim. Accept no one's definition
of your life; define yourself."

HARVEY FIERSTEIN

"Most people have to talk so they won't hear."

MAY SARTON

"One must think like a hero to behave like
a merely decent human being."

MAY SARTON

"A garden is always a series of losses set
against a few triumphs, like life itself."

MAY SARTON

"Fuck today, it's tomorrow."

FREDDIE MERCURY

"I always knew I was a star. And now,
the rest of the world seems to agree with me."

FREDDIE MERCURY

"People are always asking me what my lyrics mean.
Well I say what any decent poet would say if you
dared ask him to analyze his work:
if you see it, darling, then it's there."

FREDDIE MERCURY

"The hardest thing to learn was
the least complicated."

INDIGO GIRLS

"It is a cruel jest to say to a bootless man that he
ought to lift himself by his own bootstraps."

MARTIN LUTHER KING, JR.

"The narrower a man's mind, the broader
his statements."

CHARLES DICKENS

"And the day came when the risk it took
to remain closed in a bud became more painful
than the risk it took to blossom."

ANAÏS NIN

"There is probably no heterosexual alive who is
not preoccupied with his latent homosexuality."

NORMAN MAILER

"Everybody loves you when they are about to cum."

MADONNA

"In an expanding universe, time is on the side of the
outcast. Those who once inhabited the suburbs of
human contempt find that without changing their
address they eventually live in the metropolis."

QUENTIN CRISP

"I'm homosexual . . .
How and why are idle questions. It's a little like
wanting to know why my eyes are green."

JEAN GENET

"If God had wanted me otherwise,
He would have created me otherwise."

JOHANN WOLFGANG VON GOETHE

"Everybody winds up kissing the
wrong person good night."

ANDY WARHOL

"The human body is the best picture
of the human soul."

LUDWIG WITTGENSTEIN

"There are remarks that sow and remarks that reap."

LUDWIG WITTGENSTEIN

"Life is a moderately good play with a
badly written third act."

TRUMAN CAPOTE

"It always seemed to me a bit pointless to disapprove of homosexuality. It's like disapproving of rain."

FRANCIS MAUDE

"All men dream; but not equally. Those who dream by night in the dusty recesses of their minds wake in the day to find that it was vanity; but the dreamers of the day are dangerous men, for they may act out their dreams with open eyes, to make it possible."

T.E. LAWRENCE
(Lawrence of Arabia)

"The weak are more likely to make the strong weak than the strong are likely to make the weak strong."

MARLENE DIETRICH

"You do teach judgmental people how to be tolerant . . . . But you do it by setting an example, by tolerating them."

MICHAEL ALIG

"It is cruel, you know, that music
should beso beautiful. It has the beauty
of loneliness and of pain: of strength and freedom.
The beauty of disappointment and never-satisfied
love. The cruel beauty of nature, and
everlasting beauty of monotony."

BENJAMIN BRITTEN

"Gayness is a non-issue."

SANDRA BERNHARD

"It's been so long since I've been
that fascinated by somebody's sexuality."

SANDRA BERNHARD

"All cruel people describe themselves
as paragons of frankness!"

TENNESSEE WILLIAMS

"For time is the longest distance
between two places."

TENNESSEE WILLIAMS

"Think twice before burdening a friend with a secret."

MARLENE DIETRICH

"In memory everything seems to happen to music."

TENNESSEE WILLIAMS

"Labels are for filing. Labels are for clothing.
Labels are not for people."

MARTINA NAVRATILOVA

"An operetta is simply a small and gay opera."

GUSTAV MAHLER

"My idea of feminism is self-determination,
and it's very open-ended: every woman
has the right to become herself,
and do whatever she needs to do."

ANI DIFRANCO

"We're here because we're queer
Because we're queer because we're here."

BRENDAN BEHAN

"To achieve harmony in bad taste is
the height of elegance."

JEAN GENET

"What we need is hatred. From it our ideas are born."

JEAN GENET

"Civilization is a method of living and an
attitude of equal respect for all people."

JANE ADDAMS

"Believe those who are seeking the truth.
Doubt those who find it."

ANDRÉ GIDE

"It is better to be hated for what you are than to be
loved for what you are not."

ANDRÉ GIDE

"Are you then unable to recognize unless
it has the same sound as yours?"

ANDRÉ GIDE

"Sin is whatever obscures the soul."

ANDRÉ GIDE

"To know how to free oneself is nothing; the arduous
thing is to know what to do with one's freedom."

ANDRÉ GIDE

"The color of truth is gray."

ANDRÉ GIDE

"Nothing is more fatal to happiness like the
remembrance of happiness."

ANDRÉ GIDE

"The individual never asserts himself more
than when he forgets himself."

ANDRÉ GIDE

"Society knows perfectly well how to kill a man
and has methods more subtle than death."

ANDRÉ GIDE

"We are all inclined to judge ourselves by our ideals;
others by their acts."

HAROLD NICOLSON

"One is not born a genius, one becomes a genius."

SIMONE DE BEAUVOIR

"That a whole part of the middle class detests
me. . . is utterly normal. I would be troubled
if the contrary were true."

SIMONE DE BEAUVOIR

"All oppression creates a state of war."

SIMONE DE BEAUVOIR

"I don't remember deciding to become a writer.
You decide to become a dentist or a postman.
For me, writing is like being gay. You finally
admit that this is who you are, you come out
and hope that no one runs away. "

MARK HADDON

"I remember how being young and black and gay
and lonely felt. A lot of it was fine, feeling
I had the truth and the light and the key,
but a lot of it was purely hell."

AUDRE LORDE

"A gay man has no business leading
on a heterosexual woman."

LORNA LUFT

"Rock Hudson let his gay agent marry him off to
his secretary because he didn't want people
to get the right idea."

ANTHONY PERKINS

"No, I've never thought that I was gay. And that's not
something you think. It's something you know."

ROBERT PLANT

"Every gay and lesbian person who has been lucky
enough to survive the turmoil of growing up is a
survivor. Survivors always have an obligation to
those who will face the same challenges."

BOB PARIS

"I just wish more of my fellow queers would come out sometimes. It's nice out here, you know?"

ELTON JOHN

"If adjustment is necessary, it should be made primarily with regard to the position the homosexual occupies in present-day society, and society should more often be treated than the homosexual."

HARRY BENJAMIN

"Be careful what you set your heart upon— for it will surely be yours."

JAMES BALDWIN

"Nothing is more desirable than to be released from an affliction, but nothing is more frightening than to be divested of a crutch."

JAMES BALDWIN

"Sometimes you can't see yourself clearly until you see yourself through the eyes of others."

ELLEN DEGENERES

"Because of our social circumstances, male and female are really two cultures and their life experiences are utterly different."

KATE MILLET

"A study of the history of opinion is a necessary preliminary to the emancipation of the mind."

JOHN MAYNARD KEYNES

"I do not know which makes a man more conservative—to know nothing but the present, or nothing but the past."

JOHN MAYNARD KEYNES

"Words ought to be a little wild, for they are the assaults of thoughts on the unthinking."

JOHN MAYNARD KEYNES

"Parents have to understand: if your kid isn't you, don't blame the kid."

CHASTITY BONO

"Anger, used, does not destroy. Hatred does."

AUDRE LORDE

"Your silence will not protect you."

AUDRE LORDE

"If we wait until we are unafraid to speak,
we will be speaking from our graves."

AUDRE LORDE

"Some memories are realities,
and are better than anything that can
ever happen to one again."

WILLA CATHER

"The dead might as well try to speak
to the living as the old to the young."

WILLA CATHER

"There are only two or three human stories,
and they go on repeating themselves as fiercely
as if they had never happened before."

WILLA CATHER

"There are some things you learn best in calm,
and some in storm."

WILLA CATHER

"People like to think they can spot a gay person as
opposed to a straight person because it makes them
feel a little more defined in themselves."

GEORGE MICHAEL

"I've wondered what my sexuality might be, but I've
never wondered whether it was acceptable or not."

GEORGE MICHAEL

"How is it that so often . . . I get the feeling I've
worked hard to learn something I already know,
or knew, once."

LINDA ELLERBEE

"The only interesting answers are those
that destroy the questions."

SUSAN SONTAG

"What is the most beautiful in virile men is something feminine; what is most beautiful in feminine women is something masculine."

SUSAN SONTAG

"Books are funny little portable pieces of thought."

SUSAN SONTAG

"Though collecting quotations could be considered as merely an ironic mimetism—victimless collecting, as it were . . . in a world that is well on its way to becoming one vast quarry, the collector becomes someone engaged in a pious work of salvage. The course of modern history having already sapped the traditions and shattered the living wholes in which precious objects once found their place, the collector may now in good conscience go about excavating the choicer, more emblematic fragments."

SUSAN SONTAG

GAYS OF YORE

GREAT QUEER

MINDS HAVE BEEN MUSING SINCE FOREVER.

OR, WAIT, GREAT QUEER MUSES HAVE BEEN . . .

IN ANY CASE, OUR BROTHERS AND SISTERS

OF OLDE HAVE SPOKEN THEIR FAIR SHARE OF

WISDOM OVER THE CENTURIES. THOUGH THE

THOUGHTS HEREIN MAY NOT BE ABOUT THE

EXPERIENCE OF BEING GAY, IT'S IMPORTANT TO

GIVE OUR ANCIENT BRETHREN THEIR DUE—AND

INTRIGUING TO HEAR THE THOUGHTS OF THOSE

WHO CAME BEFORE US.

"Love is a serious mental disease."

PLATO

"Wherever it has been established that it is shameful
to be involved with sexual relationships with men,
that is due to evil on the part of the rulers, and to
cowardice on the part of the governed."

PLATO

"There is no such thing as a lover's oath."

PLATO

"Wise men talk because they have
something to say; fools, because they
have to say something."

PLATO

"Everything that deceives may be
said to enchant."

PLATO

"There is just
one life for
each of us:
our own."

EURIPIDES

"It's a good thing to be foolishly gay once in a while."

HORACE

"Hasten slowly."

AUGUSTUS CAESAR

"He is every woman's man and every man's woman."

GAIUS SCRIBONIUS CURIO
on Julius Caesar

"I came, I saw, I conquered."

JULIUS CAESAR

"All bad precedents begin as justifiable measures."

JULIUS CAESAR

"When she left, she wept a great deal; she said to me, 'This parting must be endured, Sappho. I go unwillingly.' I said, 'Go, and be happy but remember (you know well) whom you leave shackled by love.'"

SAPPHO

"Life itself is the most wonderful fairy tale."

HANS CHRISTIAN ANDERSEN

"Being born in a duck yard does not matter,
if onlyyou are hatched from a swan's egg."

HANS CHRISTIAN ANDERSEN

"Enjoy life. There's plenty of time to be dead."

HANS CHRISTIAN ANDERSEN

"The art of procreation and the members
employed therein are so repulsive, that if
it were not for the beauty of the faces and the
adornments of the actors and the pent-up impulse,
nature would lose the human species."

LEONARDO DA VINCI

"The function of muscle is to pull
and not to push, except in the case
of the genitals and the tongue."

LEONARDO DA VINCI

"Intellectual passion dries out sensuality."

LEONARDO DA VINCI

"Even if you are divine,
you don't disdain male consorts."

MICHELANGELO

"Trifles make perfection,
but perfection is no trifle."

MICHELANGELO

"What feeds me destroys me."

CHRISTOPHER MARLOWE

"Yet let me kiss my lord before I die,
And let me die with kissing of my lord."

CHRISOPHER MARLOWE

"Accursed be he that first invented war."

CHRISTOPHER MARLOWE

"Money can't buy love, but it
improves your bargaining position."

CHRISTOPHER MARLOWE

"Hope is a good breakfast, but it is a bad supper."

FRANCIS BACON

"Riches are a good handmaiden, but a poor mistress."

FRANCIS BACON

"I will never be an old man.
To me, old age is always 15 years older than I am."

FRANCIS BACON

"It is impossible to love and to be wise."

FRANCIS BACON

"Love is
a cunning
weaver of
fantasies and
fables."

SAPPHO

"Knowledge is power."

FRANCIS BACON

"Money is like manure, of very little use
except it be spread."

FRANCIS BACON

"Nature is often hidden, sometimes overcome,
seldom extinguished."

FRANCIS BACON

"People have discovered that they can fool the devil;
but they can't fool the neighbors."

FRANCIS BACON

"Truth is so hard to tell, it sometimes
needs fiction to make it plausible."

FRANCIS BACON

"The unexamined life is not worth living."

SOCRATES

"As to marriage or celibacy, let a man take which course he will, he will be sure to repent."

SOCRATES

"Call no man unhappy until he is married."

SOCRATES

"Beauty is a short-lived tyranny."

SOCRATES

"Remember upon the conduct of each depends the fate of all.

ALEXANDER THE GREAT

"Who would give a law to lovers? Love is unto itself a higher law."

BOETHIUS

"One of the penalties for refusing to participate in politics is that you end up being governed by your inferiors."

PLATO

F.O.Q. (FRIENDS OF QUEERS)

WE'VE ALL BEEN

AROUND THE BLOCK ENOUGH TIMES TO KNOW

THAT WE'RE OFTEN VERY MUCH ON OUR OWN,

BEING HOMOSEXUAL. BUT HAPPILY THERE ARE

THE FRIENDS OF QUEERS, THOSE COMPANIONS,

COHORTS, AND CAVORTERS WHO UNDERSTAND

THAT WE'RE GAY, THEY'RE NOT, BUT THERE'S

A TWAIN WHERE WE BOTH CAN MEET. SOME

QUOTED HERE ARE AVID SUPPORTERS, SOME

MERELY OFFER KIND WORDS (ONE IS EVEN

A CARTOON CHARACTER), BUT THEY ALL

UNDERSTAND OUR DIFFERENTNESS—AND OUR

SIMILARITIES. A TIP OF THE HAT TO ALL THOSE

WHO MARCH BESIDE US.

"Friendship is born at that moment when
one person says to another, "What! You too?
I thought I was the only one!"

C.S. LEWIS

"From a religious point of view,
if God had thought homosexuality is a sin,
he would not have created gay people."

HOWARD DEAN

"I'm not bad, I'm just drawn that way."

JESSICA RABBIT
in Who Framed Roger Rabbit

"I think you are wonderful and charming,
and if I should ever change from liking girls better,
you would be my first thought."

HUMPHREY BOGART *to Noel Coward*

"I think everybody in their career needs to play a
lesbian once—even if you're a man!"

KRISTIN CHENOWETH

"All the world is queer save thee and me.
And even thou art a little queer."

SIR ROBERT OWEN

"I cannot and will not cut my conscience
to fit this year's fashions."

LILLIAN HELLMAN

"All parents should be aware that when they mock or
curse gay people, they may be mocking
or cursing their own child."

ANNA QUINDLEN

"Without deviation from the norm,
progress is not possible."

FRANK ZAPPA

"Sweet boy, gentle boy, Don't be ashamed,
you are mine forever: The same rebellious fire
is in both of us. We are living one life. I am not
afraid of mockery: Between us, the two have
become one. We are precisely like a
double nut under a single shell."

ALEXANDER PUSHKIN

"God has given you one face, and you
make yourself another."

WILLIAM SHAKESPEARE

"I like my beers cold and my homosexuals flaming."

HOMER SIMPSON

"Law and justice are not always the same."

GLORIA STEINEM

"If your plane was hijacked, who would you rather
sit next to? Righteous reverends who will sit back
and say 'This is God's punishment for gay Teletubbies,'
or the gay rugby player who lays down his life
to save others?"

SCOTT SIMON

"No self-respecting gay guy would have ever made
some of the hair and clothing choices
I am still trying to live down."

DAVID COPPERFIELD

"I look ahead to the day when we won't think
of anyone as gay or straight altogether.
The fewer labels the better."

GEORGE WEINBERG

"Be who you are and say what you feel,
because those who mind don't matter and
those who matter don't mind."

DR. SEUSS

"You could move."

ABIGAIL VAN BUREN, *("Dear Abby")*
in response to a reader who complained
that a gay couple was moving in
across the street and wanted to know
what he could do to improve
the quality of the neighborhood.

"If I were gay, life would be a lot simpler.
I'm kind of annoyed that I'm not."

GRACE SLICK

"I'm for human lib, the liberation of all people, not
just black people or female people or gay people."

RICHARD PRYOR

"Let's make a law that gay people can have birthdays,
but straight people get more cake—you know,
to send the right message to kids."

BILL MAHER

"Gay people are the sweetest, kindest,
most artistic, warmest, and most thoughtful people
in the world. And since the beginning of time
all they've ever been is kicked."

LITTLE RICHARD

"We must make it clear that a platform of
'I hate gay men and women' is not a way to
become president of the United States."

JIMMY CARTER

The Portable Queer

Q

GAY ICONS

WHO BETTER

TO QUOTE (OR EVEN MISQUOTE) THAN THE

STRAIGHT GAL-PALS WE HOLD SO DEAR? CHER,

ZSA ZSA, BETTE (EITHER OR BOTH OF THEM!)—

THE WICKED WOMEN WHO ALWAYS SEEM TO

HAVE LIFE BY THE BALLS AND THE PERFECT

COMEBACK TO MATCH. IS IT THE HAIRDOS, THE

SHOES, THE CIGARETTE HOLDERS? SOMETIMES

YOU JUST HAVE TO ASK YOURSELF: WHAT ARE

THEY TAKING THAT MAKE THEM SO MUCH

GAYER THAN US?

"Deep down, I'm pretty superficial."

AVA GARDNER

"I am a marvelous housekeeper.
Every time I leave a man I keep his house."

ZSA ZSA GABOR

"How many husbands have I had?
You mean apart from my own?"

ZSA ZSA GABOR

"I may not be a great actress but I've become the
greatest at screen orgasms. Ten seconds of heavy
breathing, roll your head from side to side, simulate
a slight asthma attack, and die a little."

CANDICE BERGEN

"Filipinos want beauty. I have to look beautiful
so that the poor Filipinos will have a star to
look at from their slums."

IMELDA MARCOS

"It was God who made me so beautiful.
If I weren't, then I'd be a teacher."

LINDA EVANGELISTA

"I've been through it all, baby.
I'm Mother Courage."

ELIZABETH TAYLOR

"There are two reasons why I'm in show business,
and I'm standing on both of them."

BETTY GRABLE

"Personally I know nothing about sex
because I've always been married."

ZSA ZSA GABOR

"You can wait for the right guy to come along—
but in the meantime you can have a wonderful time
with all the wrong ones."

CHER

"I think that the longer I look good,
the better gay men feel."

CHER

"The trouble with some women is that
they get all excited about nothing—
and then marry him."

CHER

"When I get down on my knees, it is not to pray."

MADONNA

"They don't call it a 'job' for nothing."

KIM CATTRALL
as "Samantha" on Sex in the City

"Always be a first-rate version of yourself,
instead of a second-rate version of somebody else."

JUDY GARLAND

"The problem with beauty is that it's like
being born rich and getting poorer."

JOAN COLLINS

"Sex appeal is 50 per cent what you've got and 50 per cent what people think you've got."

SOPHIA LOREN

"A sure way to lose happiness is to want it at the expense of everything else."

BETTE DAVIS

"Gay Liberation? I ain't against it; it's just that there's nothing in it for me."

BETTE DAVIS

"It's a helluva start, being able to recognize what makes you happy."

LUCILLE BALL

"What I am is a humanist before anything— before I'm a Jew, before I'm black, before I'm a woman. And my beliefs are for the human race—they don't exclude anyone."

WHOOPI GOLDBERG

"Normal is in the eye of the beholder."

WHOOPI GOLDBERG

"I am where I am because I believe
in all possibilities."

WHOOPI GOLDBERG

"A hard man is good to find."

MAE WEST

"A man has one hundred dollars and you leave him
with two dollars, that's subtraction."

MAE WEST

"Anything worth doing is worth doing slowly."

MAE WEST

"Between two evils, I always pick the one
I never tried before."

MAE WEST

"I used to be Snow White but I drifted."

MAE WEST

"I wrote the story myself. It's about a girl who
lost her reputation and never missed it."

MAE WEST

"It is better to be looked over than overlooked."

MAE WEST

"Sex is emotion in motion."

MAE WEST

"She's the kind of girl who climbed
the ladder of success wrong by wrong."

MAE WEST

"To err is human, but it feels divine."

MAE WEST

"Too much of a good thing can be wonderful."

MAE WEST

"When I'm good, I'm very good.
But when I'm bad I'm better."

MAE WEST

"You only live once, but if you do it right,
once is enough."

MAE WEST

"Give a man a free hand and he'll
run it all over you."

MAE WEST

"I only like two kinds of men,
domestic and imported."

MAE WEST

"It's not the having, it's the getting."

ELIZABETH TAYLOR

"If it weren't for homosexuals,
there'd be no Hollywood."

ELIZABETH TAYLOR

"I feel like a million tonight—
but one at a time."

BETTE MIDLER

THE LAST WORD

"I love quotations because it is a joy to find thoughts one might have, beautifully expressed

with much
authority by
someone
recognized
wiser than
oneself."

MARLENE DIETRICH